HAL•LEONARD
INSTRUMENTAL
PLAY-ALONG

AUDIO ACCESS
INCLUDED

TRUMPET

A NEW MUSICAL
WICKED

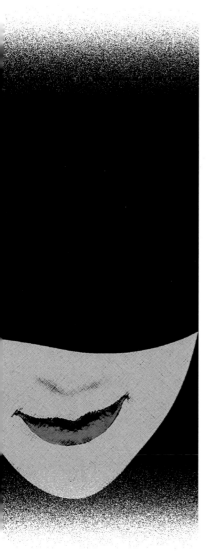

To access audio visit:
www.halleonard.com/mylibrary

Enter Code
4060-1685-4221-1513

T0056193

ISBN 978-1-4234-4970-6

HAL•LEONARD®
CORPORATION
7777 W. BLUEMOUND RD. P.O. BOX 13819 MILWAUKEE, WI 53213

Visit Hal Leonard Online at
www.halleonard.com

AS LONG AS YOU'RE MINE

Music and Lyrics by
STEPHEN SCHWARTZ

TRUMPET

DANCING THROUGH LIFE

TRUMPET

Words and Music by
STEPHEN SCHWARTZ

DEFYING GRAVITY

TRUMPET

Words and Music by
STEPHEN SCHWARTZ

FOR GOOD

TRUMPET

Words and Music by
STEPHEN SCHWARTZ

I COULDN'T BE HAPPIER

TRUMPET

Words and Music by
STEPHEN SCHWARTZ

I'M NOT THAT GIRL

TRUPPET

Words and Music by
STEPHEN SCHWARTZ

NO GOOD DEED

TRUMPET

Words and Music by
STEPHEN SCHWARTZ

ONE SHORT DAY

TRUMPET

Music and Lyrics by
STEPHEN SCHWARTZ

POPULAR

TRUMPET

Words and Music by
STEPHEN SCHWARTZ

WHAT IS THIS FEELING?

Words and Music by
STEPHEN SCHWARTZ

TRUMPET

THE WIZARD AND I

TRUMPET

Words and Music by
STEPHEN SCHWARTZ

21

WONDERFUL

TRUMPET

Music and Lyrics by
STEPHEN SCHWARTZ

NO ONE MOURNS THE WICKED

TRUMPET

Words and Music by
STEPHEN SCHWARTZ